HAL•LEONARD
INSTRUMENTAL
PLAY-ALONG

AUDIO ACCESS INCLUDED

PLAYBACK+
Speed • Pitch • Balance • Loop

TENOR SAX

Disney • PIXAR

COCO

T0084977

Audio arrangements by Peter Deneff

To access audio visit:
www.halleonard.com/mylibrary
Enter Code
1846-6224-8550-9767

ISBN 978-1-5400-2136-6

HAL•LEONARD®
7777 W. Bluemound Rd. P.O. Box 13819 Milwaukee, WI 53213

In Australia Contact:
Hal Leonard Australia Pty. Ltd.
4 Lentara Court
Cheltenham, Victoria, 3192 Australia
Email: ausadmin@halleonard.com.au

Visit Hal Leonard Online at
www.halleonard.com

EVERYONE KNOWS JUANITA

from COCO

TENOR SAX

Music by GERMAINE FRANCO
Lyrics by ADRIAN MOLINA

MUCH NEEDED ADVICE

from COCO

TENOR SAX

Music by MICHAEL GIACCHINO
and GERMAINE FRANCO
Lyrics by ADRIAN MOLINA

LA LLORONA
from COCO

TENOR SAX

Traditional Mexican Folksong
Arranged by GERMAINE FRANCO

2.
(♪ = ♪)
mf
f
1.
2.
ff

PROUD CORAZÓN

from COCO

TENOR SAX

Music by GERMAINE FRANCO
Lyrics by ADRIAN MOLINA

REMEMBER ME

(Ernesto de la Cruz)

from COCO

TENOR SAX

Words and Music by KRISTEN ANDERSON-LOPEZ
and ROBERT LOPEZ

UN POCO LOCO

from COCO

TENOR SAX

Music by GERMAINE FRANCO
Lyrics by ADRIAN MOLINA

2
ff

THE WORLD ES MI FAMILIA

from COCO

TENOR SAX

Music by GERMAINE FRANCO
Lyrics by ADRIAN MOLINA

Moderately fast, in 2